SERIES EDITOR   DAVID SALARIYA
EDITOR   APRIL McCROSKIE
CONSULTANT   DR GERALD LEGG

W FRANKLIN WATTS

First published in 1996
by Franklin Watts
a division of the Watts Publishing Group Ltd
96 Leonard Street
London EC2A 4XD

This edition published 2000

ISBN 0 7496 3809 5
Dewey Classification 574.5

© THE SALARIYA BOOK COMPANY LTD MCMXCVI

Printed in Belgium

A CIP catalogue record for this book is available from the British Library.

rainforest

Written by
PENNY CLARKE

Illustrated by
CAROLYN SCRACE

Series Created & Designed by
DAVID SALARIYA

FRANKLIN WATTS
LONDON • SYDNEY

Rainforests have more wildlife than any other habitat. Scientists believe that one hectare of the South American rainforest will contain 42,000 species of insect (including 50 species of ant), up to 750 species of tree, 1500 other plant species, as well as the many birds and animals. One reason for this is the height of the rainforest trees. While most are around 50 metres high, some palms reach 108 metres. A rainforest has many layers and, as you will discover from this book, different plants and animals live in the different layers.

Boa constrictor

Spider monkey

Many different kinds of tree grow in rainforests. They provide food and shelter for hundreds of species of animals and smaller plants.

Keel-billed toucan

Toucans live in South American rainforests. They eat fruit, which they pick with their big bills.

A rainforest is an area of dense tropical forest, where the temperature and rainfall are high and steady all year. From above, a rainforest looks like a green sea with treetops stretching as far as you can see. This is called the canopy. The canopy is high above the ground, because many rainforest trees are very tall. The only gaps are where rivers flow through the rainforest.

Claws

The three-toed sloth moves very slowly, holding on to tree branches with its long, curved claws.

Creeper or liana

Tree porcupine

The tamandua also spends most of its life in the trees. It feeds on ants, catching them on its long, sticky tongue.

Tamandua

Tongue

Ants' nest

Rainforests occur in South America, Africa and Asia. Most are between the Tropic of Cancer north of the Equator and the Tropic of Capricorn south of the Equator. The largest area of rainforest in the world is in Brazil, in South America. Rainforests need at least 200 cm of rainfall spread evenly throughout the year, and a temperature of 26°C. It is the warmth and damp that make trees and plants flourish.

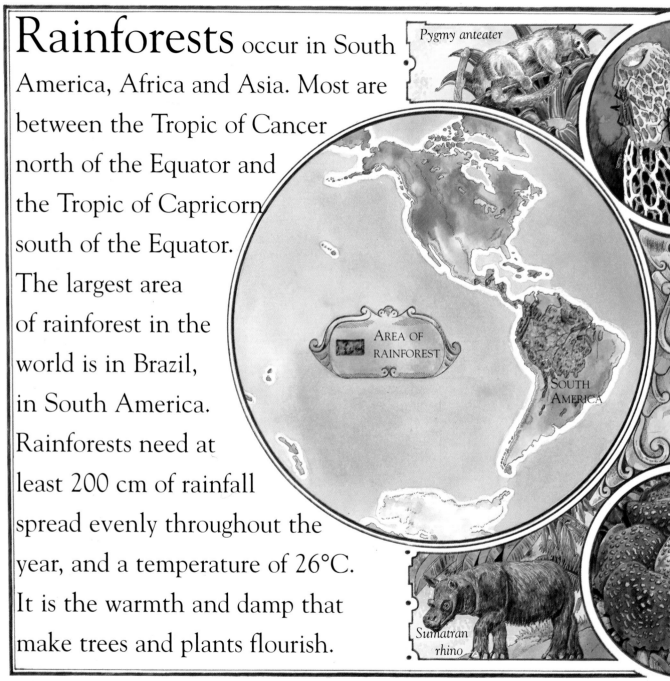

Pygmy anteater

AREA OF RAINFOREST

SOUTH AMERICA

Sumatran rhino

Caterpillar from New Guinea

Tarsier

AFRICA

ASIA

NEW GUINEA

Giant anteater

Mandrill

Tarsiers live in the rainforests of Asia. Their large eyes help them see in the dark. This shows shows they are nocturnal—hunting for their insect food at night.

Centre: Top, Maiden's veil stinkhorn
Bottom, Rafflesia

Count Raggi's bird of paradise

Birds of paradise are found in the rainforests of Asia. The rainforests are so dense scientists are not sure how many species there are. About a hundred years ago the birds were hunted for their bright feathers. They are now protected.

11

Without

trees there would be no rainforests. But without high rainfall and a hot, steady temperature there would be no trees to form a rainforest. Just as the trees need the right climate, everything else in the rainforest needs the trees in some way. And the trees themselves need birds, animals and insects to pollinate their flowers and spread their seeds. Scientists call this interdependence.

Tree canopy

Bromeliad

Mosses

12

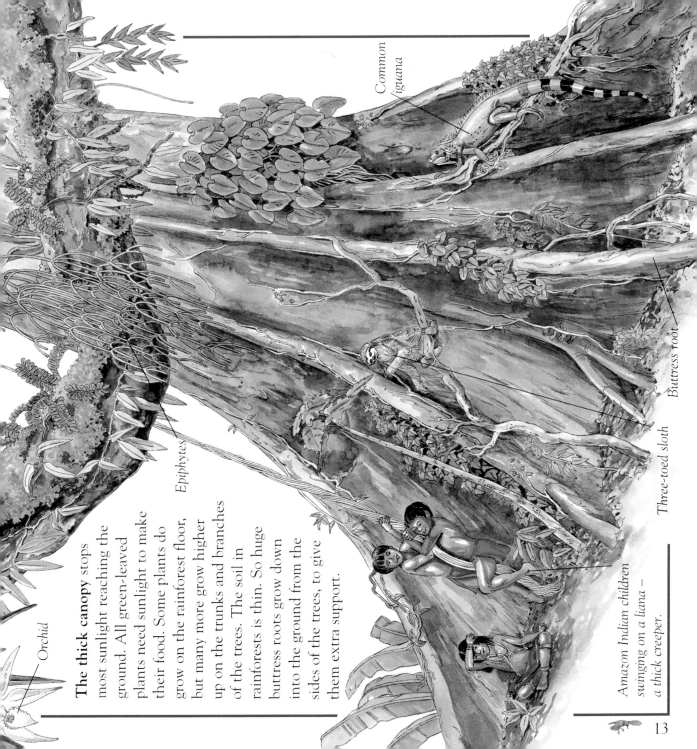

Common iguana

Orchid

Epiphytes

The thick canopy stops most sunlight reaching the ground. All green-leaved plants need sunlight to make their food. Some plants do grow on the rainforest floor, but many more grow higher up on the trunks and branches of the trees. The soil in rainforests is thin. So huge buttress roots grow down into the ground from the sides of the trees, to give them extra support.

Buttress root

Three-toed sloth

Amazon Indian children swinging on a liana – a thick creeper.

13

Golden potto

The **golden potto** of the African rainforest feeds at night on insects and fruit.

Collared sunbird

The trees of the

rainforest are so tall that conditions in the canopy are different to those on the ground. The canopy gets all the sun and rain. The forest floor is rather dim and fairly dry. Between the canopy and floor it is different again. Many plants and animals live in just one of the layers or strata. Some frogs live on the forest floor, but others live in pools of water in plant leaves high above ground. Mandrills only use the trees to sleep in, while diana monkeys live only near the canopy.

All these creatures live in the rainforests of Africa. Turn the page to see a South American rainforest.

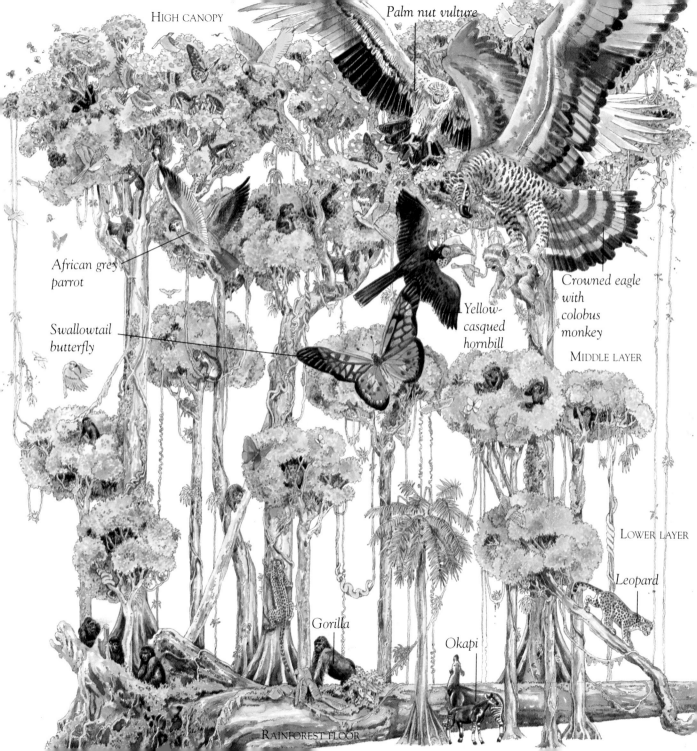

HIGH CANOPY

Palm nut vulture

African grey parrot

Crowned eagle with colobus monkey

Swallowtail butterfly

Yellow-casqued hornbill

MIDDLE LAYER

LOWER LAYER

Leopard

Gorilla

Okapi

RAINFOREST FLOOR

Flying roots grow out from a tree's trunk about 6 to 9 metres above the ground. They root some way from the base of the tree, making it more stable.

Prehensile tail able to grasp things

Pangolin

Buttress roots

Okapi

Gorilla

Spitting cobra about to attack

Parasol fungi

Young gorilla

Forest millipede

The spitting cobra 'spits' poison through its fangs at an attacker. The poison can cause blindness if it gets into the attacker's eyes.

Baby hoatzin

Baby hoatzins cling
to branches with
their wing claws.

Anacondas can grow
to 11.4 metres long.
They swim well.

The rainforest of South

America is drained by the River Amazon
and its many tributaries. They flow from
the Andes mountains across the lowlands of
Brazil to reach the Atlantic. The rivers used
to be the highways of the region. The waters
and banks of the rivers are rich in wildlife.

*Giant
otter*

Anaconda

Swordtail

Electric eel

Electric eels stun
their prey with an
electric shock.

Terrapin

Neon tetras

The Brazilian
tapir is a strong
swimmer.

Brazilian tapir

A female alligator
builds a nest of
mud and rotting
plants. She lays
her eggs here.

Female alligator

Paca

Scarlet ibis

Barbel

Angelfish

Catfish find their
prey in the muddy
rivers with their
sensitive barbels.

Catfish

21

Blossom bat

Like most bats, blossom bats come out to feed at dusk.

Green tree python

Blossom bats pollinate many rainforest trees in New Guinea. The trees flower at dusk, when the bats come out to feed.

Above the rainforest floor, but below the canopy, is a world on its own. Leaves fall into crevices in tree bark. They rot and provide homes for worms and fungi that normally live on the ground. Other crevices give root holds for plants like bromeliads. Water collects in their leaves where tree frogs lay their eggs. The green tree python of New Guinea moves quietly through the trees hunting insects, birds and mammals.

Green tree frog

Many large moths and butterflies live in rainforests. The Hercules moth of New Guinea has a wingspan of 25 cm.

Hercules moth

Goodfellow's tree kangaroo travels through New Guinea's rainforests, leaping up to 7 metres from one tree to another.

Liana

The spotted cuscus lives in New Guinea. It hunts at night.

Sugar glider

Sugar gliders leap from one tree to another by stretching out their legs. An extra fold of skin helps them glide safely for up to 55 metres. **Turn the page to see the hidden life of the rainforest.**

23

The king vulture feeds on dead animals, especially fish. Its excellent sense of smell helps it find food in the dense rainforest.

Only king vultures over two years old have brightly coloured heads.

Ruby topaz hummingbird

Fragrant orchid

The canopy is

the warmest, wettest and lightest part of the rainforest. More creatures live in the canopy than in any other part of the rainforest. The different plants provide food for them all. Hummingbirds sip nectar from brilliantly coloured flowers. Monkeys search for fruit, insects and birds' eggs. Groups of macaws feed on fruits, seeds and berries, flying off noisily if they are disturbed.

26

The bright blue wings of the Morpho butterfly glitter in the sunlight of the canopy.

Macaw

Morpho butterfly

Skeleton butterfly

Pair of squirrel monkeys

Uakari and young

Woolly monkey

Rainforests have life cycles.
Their soil is poor, so it is important that anything dead is broken down quickly. This releases nutrients into the soil where they are absorbed by the tree roots. The nutrients help the trees produce the flowers and fruit on which many creatures feed. These, in turn, are food for the hunters.

Asian leopard cat

Tree shrew

Termites

Indian tiger

Fallen
forest giant

When a rainforest tree falls, it
brings down many other trees.
More light and rain can reach the
forest floor. This helps young trees
to grow, replacing the fallen ones.

Butterflies flock to
the new forest clearing

A lar gibbon clutches
an insect it had caught
just before it, in turn,
was caught by the
Indian python.

Army ants

Indian python

Lar gibbon

Insect

29

Jackson's chameleon

Camouflaged skin

Species of plants or animals cannot survive if the members do not produce young. Adult animals of the same species must mate for the species to survive. But there are many dangers in the rainforest. To try to survive, rainforest creatures defend themselves in different ways. Some confuse their attackers by looking like something else. Others are so well camouflaged the animal they are hunting does not see them.

A chameleon's skin cells expand and contract to change colour. This camouflages the animal before it shoots out its long tongue to trap the prey.

30

Chameleon's long tongue

The bright colour of the poison dart frog warns other creatures to avoid it – it is poisonous. Many dangerous creatures use this defence.

Fer-de-lance waiting for prey

Poison dart frog

Pangolins roll into a ball. Unrolled (*page 19*), they are an easy prey, but once rolled up not even a leopard's strong claws can prise them open.

Tree pangolin

Mantis gripping prey

Imitating something else is a good defence, especially if the creature imitated is not good to eat. Some mantises imitate dead leaves. Can you find it here?

The rosy periwinkle from Madagascar gives medicine to help treat a cancer called leukaemia.

Quinine, the first treatment for malaria, a tropical disease, came from the bark of the cinchona tree of South America.

Rainforests are very important to the earth. All mammals breathe in oxygen, but breathe out carbon dioxide gas (CO_2), which is poisonous to breathe in. Plants absorb carbon dioxide, so rainforests absorb huge amounts of it. This is important because CO_2 is a 'greenhouse gas'. This means that too much CO_2 in the earth's atmosphere will raise the temperature and increase global warming. Global warming will speed up the melting of ice in the Arctic and Antarctic. This melted ice will raise sea levels and will flood low-lying parts of the world.

Mosquitoes spread malaria among humans.

Skin

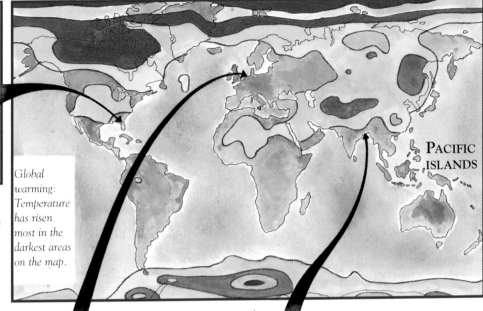

FLORIDA

Global warming: Temperature has risen most in the darkest areas on the map.

PACIFIC ISLANDS

Low-lying parts of the world will be flooded if global warming increases. Areas particularly at risk are Florida in the USA, the Netherlands in north-west Europe, Bangladesh in the Indian subcontinent and the Pacific islands.

NETHERLANDS

Much of the Netherlands is below sea level. It is only protected from the North Sea by strong sea walls.

BANGLADESH

The huge delta of the River Ganges forms a large part of Bangladesh. If the sea level rises all that land will disappear.

Collecting rubber

Rubber is the sap of a tree first found in the Amazon rainforest. Imagine life without rubber.

Wild pineapples still grow in the rainforests.

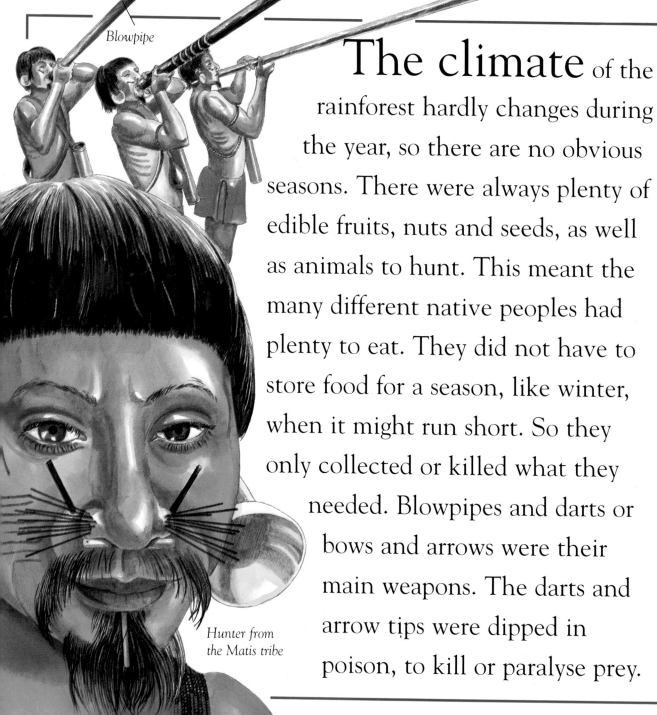

Blowpipe

Hunter from
the Matis tribe

The climate of the rainforest hardly changes during the year, so there are no obvious seasons. There were always plenty of edible fruits, nuts and seeds, as well as animals to hunt. This meant the many different native peoples had plenty to eat. They did not have to store food for a season, like winter, when it might run short. So they only collected or killed what they needed. Blowpipes and darts or bows and arrows were their main weapons. The darts and arrow tips were dipped in poison, to kill or paralyse prey.

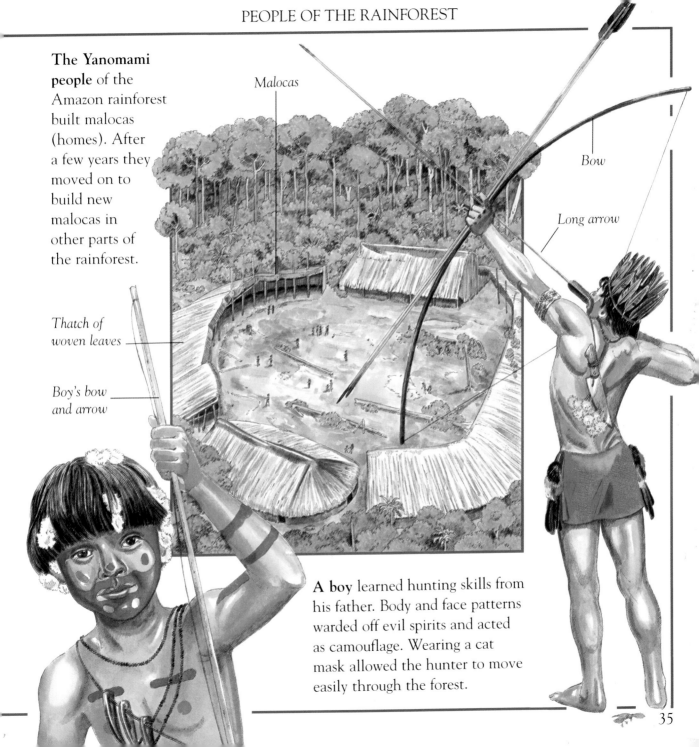

The Yanomami people of the Amazon rainforest built malocas (homes). After a few years they moved on to build new malocas in other parts of the rainforest.

Malocas

Bow

Long arrow

Thatch of woven leaves

Boy's bow and arrow

A boy learned hunting skills from his father. Body and face patterns warded off evil spirits and acted as camouflage. Wearing a cat mask allowed the hunter to move easily through the forest.

Rainforests are under threat. Many countries with rainforests are poor. Their governments see the forests as areas where nothing useful grows. They think the land should be used to rear cattle or grow crops. But the soil is thin. If the trees are cut down, the soil is soon washed away. Where will the crops grow then? Even if crops are planted the soil is so poor they do not grow well. Rainforests affect the world's weather. Trees release moisture into the air. If there are no trees to do this, rainfall levels drop and the world climate changes.

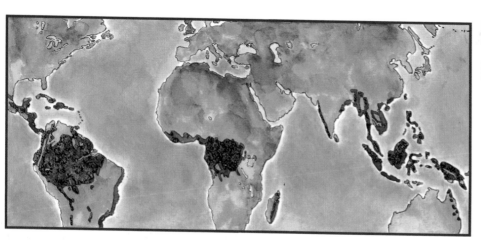

 RAINFOREST

 AREA LOST EACH YEAR

The soil washed away from cleared rainforests can be seen miles out at sea.

Once rainforest is cut down it cannot grow again. It is lost forever, and so is everything that lived in it. Scientists are sure that there are still many undiscovered plants and animals in the world's rainforests.

Quetzal

You can help by supporting environmental organizations. And **never** buy anything like a plant, bird, animal or wooden object, that may have come from the rainforests.

Crashing forest tree

Roads and lorries bring more destruction and pollution.

Chainsaws make felling trees easy.

USEFUL WORDS

Barbel Sensitive 'whiskers' around the mouths of fish like catfish.

Bromeliad Plant of the pineapple family, with stiff, leathery leaves.

Camouflage Markings or colouring on a creature that help it blend with its surroundings.

Carbon dioxide A gas that we give off when we breathe. It occurs naturally in the environment. Trees absorb it.

Epiphytes Plants that grow on other plants, but do them no harm.

Epiphytes get water from rain trapped in their leaves, not through their roots like other plants.

Habitat Wherever a plant or animal lives naturally.

Interdependence Depending on one another.

Mammal Animal fed on its mother's milk when it is young.

Nutrient A substance that provides nourishment.

Paralyse To make something powerless.

Pollination Exchange of pollen between flowering plants. If the flower is not pollinated, it cannot produce fruit or seeds.

Prehensile Able to grasp things.

Prey Creature that is hunted for food.

Species A group of animals or plants that look alike, live in the same way and produce young that do the same.

Tributary A stream or river that flows into a larger one.

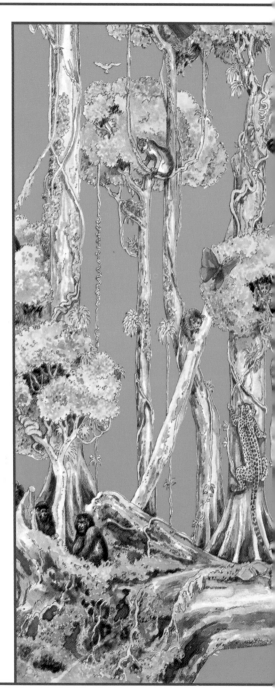

INDEX